FASHIONS FROM
INDIA

Tom Tierney

DOVER PUBLICATIONS, INC.
Mineola, New York

D1361295

Bibliographical Note

Fashions from India is a new work, first published by Dover Publications, Inc., in 2003.

International Standard Book Number

ISBN-13: 978-0-486-43040-9
ISBN-10: 0-486-43040-5

Manufactured in the United States by Courier Corporation
43040502   2013
www.doverpublications.com

INTRODUCTION

Our knowledge of India's ancient dress is based on works of art, such as sculptures and paintings, that have survived over time. Since this art was almost always financed and created for the pleasure of the upper classes, our picture of ancient India's clothing is primarily the dress of the royals and their deities. Members of the subcontinent's vast and varied regional groups wear, and have worn, clothing and ornaments designed to clearly define their status in Indian society.

Two garments predominate in India: the *dhoti* for men, and the *sari* for women. These items of clothing have been the basis of Indian costume from as early as the second century B.C., and probably date back even further to prehistoric times. In early sculptured reliefs, both men and women are depicted wearing a long piece of cloth wrapped around the hips and drawn between the legs to form a series of folds down the front. The upper bodies of both men and women frequently were unclothed, although the women (and some Indian gods, as well) were often shown wearing a narrow cloth girdle around the waist. Generally, women were depicted wearing more jewelry than men, and they used head-scarves—*dopatta*—that fell to the hip. Headdresses for both men and women were quite elaborate; existing sculptures indicate that they included jeweled turbans and molded crowns.

Clothing styles of the Indian subcontinent underwent a major change in the twelfth century, when Arab Muslims conquered north and central India; they were followed in later years by the Mughals, from central Asia. Muslim religious codes required that the body be covered as much as possible, bringing about the use of the *jama,* a long-sleeved coat reaching to the knee or below, belted with a sash, and combined with wide-hipped trousers called *isar.* Another garment, the *farji,* a long, gown-like, short-sleeved coat, was worn by scholars, priests, and other high officials. Since silk was forbidden by their religious laws, Muslim men wore garments of cotton or wool, and sheer cotton became a luxury fabric. The Koran did not forbid the use of silk by women, and ladies of the court wore luxurious silks

to great advantage. The earlier Muslim woman's costume consisted of wide-topped trousers fitting snugly from calf to ankle; a long shirt-like blouse called a *kurta;* and a fitted outer jacket and dopatta. Under the rule of the emperor Akbar Rajput, a graceful new style appeared: a pleated, open-fronted skirt called a *ghaghra.* It was worn with an apron-like panel tucked into the waist to cover the front opening. The upper garment was a short-sleeved, breast-length blouse called a *choli.* To this day, the ghaghra and the choli continue to be the basic elements of the Muslim woman's dress, the apron-like panel having metamorphosed into the traditional sari, which is worn as an overgarment, with one end draped around the hips and the other draped over the shoulder and, perhaps, the head.

The Muslim rules of dress had little effect on the costume of south India. The dhoti continued to be preferred by most Hindu men, although it was forbidden by a few castes (social classes within Indian society), and the sari became the favored garment of most women. In the twentieth century, for formal or semi-formal occasions, a long, full-skirted, narrow-sleeved coat, worn over jodhpur-style trousers—sometimes called the "Nehru jacket"—was extremely popular; it even created an international fashion. Women's formal wear at the turn of the twenty-first century consists of variations of the sari and the choli, although western-ized fashions are becoming more and more invasive in the Indian fashion lexicon. Whereas clothing tradition-ally indicated the wearer's status in Indian society, many of today's women on the subcontinent express their individual taste through their dress.

Accessories play an important part in Indian cos-tume. As many of these pages reveal, jewelry can be quite opulent, ranging from chokers and chains around the neck, to dangle earrings, arm and wrist bangles, and anklets. The materials used include silver, gold, and mixed metals, often set with precious and semiprecious stones. An ornament called a *tikka* consists of a pen-dant attached to a chain worn over a woman's head; the pendant rests on the wearer's forehead.

Glossary of Indian Costume Terms

Angharka: An archaic name for the *jama*, a long-sleeved overgarment worn by Mughal men.

Chakdar jama: Four-pointed skirt worn by both men and women, introduced by the Mughals.

Chauri: Fly whisk, usually of yak tail.

Chhattar: Umbrella.

Choli: Women's traditional short-sleeved, tightly fitted, breast-length blouse, generally worn under a sari.

Chouridar: Full-legged trousers that are gathered to fit the ankle at the hemline.

Comboy: Shirt-like garment of Sri Lanka (formerly Ceylon) worn by men, women, and children; cut very full and in varying lengths, it can be draped around the body in a variety of ways.

Dhoti: Long loincloth worn by Hindu men (and by both sexes in pre-Mughal times).

Dopatta: Thin shawl of silk or muslin worn over the head and shoulders by Muslim women.

Farji: A short-sleeved long, flowing coat worn by scholars, priests, and high officials.

Fez (tarboosh): The fez was introduced into India by educator and reformer Sayyad Ahmad in the nineteenth century. The Indian tarboosh differs considerably from the original Islamic felt fez in both color and fabric.

Gadi: A cushion, used especially for royal thrones.

Ghaghra: Woman's long, open-fronted, pleated skirt introduced by the Mughals. The skirt opening was hidden by a long, apron-like panel tucked in at the waist.

Huqqa: Water pipe.

Isar: Mughal trousers, worn by both sexes; they were cut quite wide through the hip and tapered to the ankle.

Jama (Jamah): Overgarment or overdress; earliest form of a coat in India.

Jodhpurs: A style of trouser, full to the knee and tight at the ankle, named for the Indian province where they originated; westernized into riding breeches.

Kard: Persian dagger with a straight blade and hilt.

Katar: Thrusting dagger with double-edged blade and a transverse grip between two parallel bars.

Khanjar: Curved dagger, often double curved and double edged, with a pistol-grip handle.

Kirttimukha: Lion mask, a symbol of the god Shiva.

Kurta: An overshirt or tunic, worn by both sexes; today it is often seen combined with *chouridar* on women.

Mojari: Traditional Muslim slippers with pointed, upward-curving toes, worn by men of rank. Made of fine leather or expensive fabrics, mojari often were elaborately jeweled and embroidered in gold.

Morchhal: Feather fly whisk or fan.

Pagri (puggree): The turban worn by Hindu men. A large, self-draping strip of cotton, five to 25 yards long; it is wound around the head in various styles, often with one end hanging down the back.

Paijama: Long, loose trousers, usually made of a thin material; they sometimes were wound around the lower leg to form a jodhpur-like shape.

Palu: The end of a sari, which hangs from the shoulder or is draped over the head.

Purdah (parda): The veiling of women; can also refer to their confinement at home.

Pashmina: Fine Kashmiri wool used for shawls.

Patka: Sash worn by nobility.

Punjabi suit: An ensemble consisting of long, baggy pants drawn in at the ankle (*chouridar*) and a three-quarter-length tunic (*kurta*). A shawl (*dopatta*) is draped over the breast and shoulders.

Puttees: A narrow strip of cloth wound spirally around the leg from ankle to knee. The first puttees (from *patti*, the Hindu word for a strip of cloth) appeared in the Anglo-Indian army in the late nineteenth century.

Salwar: Loose pajama-like trousers, worn by women throughout India and by Punjabi men.

Sari: A piece of fabric about two to four feet wide and five to eleven yards long, generally of cotton or silk in elaborate prints and vivid colors and often shot through with metallic stripes or patterns. The sari, worn in combination with a choli and a full-length petticoat, is tucked into the waistband of the petticoat and wrapped around the waist to form a skirt; the surplus is carried up in front and draped over the shoulder and, perhaps, the head. Girls begin wearing the sari around puberty.

Sarong: A piece of fabric four to five yards long, it is wrapped around the hips and tucked into a sash, forming a draped skirt of varying length from knee to ankle. The sarong was worn by both sexes in the Malay Archipelago, Ceylon (now Sri Lanka), and some parts of India.

Sarpech: A turban ornament or brooch. The lower part is called the *arpati*, the upper the *jigha*.

Shah tus ("king's fleece"): Refers to fleece left on bushes by passing wild mountain goats; the collected wool makes the finest Kashmiri shawls and is quite expensive.

Taj: Crown; also refers to the folded cloth peak around which some turbans are wound.

Talwar: Sword with a long, curved blade.

Tikka: Pendant extending to the forehead from a chain worn over the head.

Tilaka: Mark made on the forehead of Hindus; it varies according to the sect.

Shiva and Parvati, Tenth Century

Examples of the male and female dhoti are depicted on these figures from a sculptured relief of the Chola dynasty in the tenth century. The male figure represents the god Shiva as Lingodbhava, the creator; the female is the goddess Parvati, Shiva's consort.

Mughal Rural Folk, ca. 1400s

The picture of this fifteenth-century family is based on an early manuscript. The man wears a dhoti and a shawl; his head is covered by a loosely tied turban. The woman wears a sari and carries a painted fan of soft leather.

Mughal Court Official, 1565

This Mughal dignitary wears a jama, also known as an angharka, which is edged and sashed with brocaded gold cotton fabric (a noble's sash was called a *patka*).

The official's turban is also of a brocaded gold fabric. The Hindu name for the turban is *pagri*.

Mughal Courtier, ca. 1590

This courtier was a member of the court of the Mughal emperor Akbar near the end of the sixteenth century. During this period, the Mughals introduced a four- pointed skirt called a chakdar jama, which was stiffened somewhat, allowing the lower skirt to fall in points.

Mughal Woman, ca. 1600

In a style similar to the men's, Mughal women appear to have also worn the kurta falling in points. This woman wears two shawls, or dopatta, one around her neck and the other draped over her arms. She wears armbands and wristbands, a multi-tiered necklace, and an intricate hair ornament.

Mughal Warrior, ca. 1600

A Mughal warrior is shown in service to the emperor Akbar. A horseman, he is dressed in a short, thigh-length jama worn over a long, fitted-sleeve kurta. On his wrists he wears leather wrist protectors. His shield and leggings are of padded leather, and he wears fitted trousers and soft boots, probably of felt. His helmet is made of metal and leather.

Raja of Amber and Family, ca. 1620

The Raja of Amber is shown with his wife and son, the prince. The Raja's chakdar jama skirt is made of the sheerest of cotton, denoting his high status. The dagger at his waist is called a katar. His wife is dressed in a sari and dopatta of silk and carries an ostrich feather—a *morchhal*—to shoo away flies. The prince wears a gold brocaded cap edged with pearls; pearls also appear at his wrists and ankles.

Mumtaz Mahal, ca. 1630

Based on a miniature portrait of Mumtaz Mahal, this picture shows the favorite wife of emperor Shah Jahan. Her name meant "the beauty of the palace," and Shah Jahan built the Taj Mahal as his wife's mortuary after her death. Mumtaz wears the abbreviated choli, with a sheer silk ghaghra and an embroidered apron, over her patterned trousers. She wears jewels on her feet, in addition to the many necklaces, bangles, and other accessories shown here. Her turban is wound in the taj (crown) manner.

Shah Jahan, ca. 1630

Shah Jahan was the Mughal emperor who built the Taj Mahal in tribute to his favorite wife, Mumtaz. His costume consists of a belted and sashed sheer cotton jama, or angharka, worn over isar; an embroidered short kurta; and a talwar—long, curved sword.

Madras Dancer, ca. 1640

The cotton fabrics from the Madras region are famous for their beauty and durability and often are referred to simply as "madras" (not to be confused with the East Indies "madras plaid" fabrics which are meant to fade with washing). This dancer from the Madras region wears an elaborately draped, belted sari that features an apron scarf. She wears both a tikka and tilaka.

Mughal Court Dancer, ca. 1650

This dancer is dressed in a choli, worn above a sheer ghaghra and chouridar. Her long headscarf reaches almost to her ankles; she wears arm, wrist, and ankle ornaments.

Mughal Lord, ca. 1650

A Mughal lord of the mid-seventeenth century wears a jeweled, striped turban, or pagri. The jeweled brooch decorating the turban is a sarpech. Over his jama he wears a decorative belt and a brocaded, embroidered apron. He wears gloves of soft kid, embroidered in gold at the cuffs. On his feet he wears the pointed-toe, elaborately decorated Muslim slippers called mojari, which were reserved for the males of the court; all others went barefoot.

Ali Adil-Shah II, ca. 1660

Ali Adil-Shah II, a king of Bijapur, is shown here slaying a tiger. He wears a knee-length jama over his isar; from his belt hangs an elaborately tooled arrow quiver. He has tucked a katar, or thrusting dagger, in his belt. He wears decorated mojari.

Lady of the Court, ca. 1675

This image is taken from a manuscript from the Punjab Hills, late-seventeenth century. A lady of the court is shown with her hunting rifle (women often were shown carrying guns during this period). The lady wears a choli and isar and a sheer silk kurta. A sheer, embroidered dopatta is draped over her head and shoulders.

Landowner and Farmer, ca. 1750

This picture of a landowner and a farmer is based on art in the style of the Guler region from the mid-eighteenth century. The landowner is dressed in a print jama with an embroidered sash. Across his chest he wears a scarf draped like a bandoleer. The farmer wears an abbreviated dhoti and a felt cap.

Farm Women and Child, ca. 1750

These farm women and child are pictured in a representation of the clothing style of Guler art of the mid-eighteenth century. The women wear the traditional choli and sari, and the child wears a sheer cotton kurta.

Couple from Kangra, ca. 1780

These young lovers from Kangra, a region in northern India, are figures from the art of the late-eighteenth century. The woman wears a long, pleated cotton farji over a long-sleeved shirt; she has draped a large dopatta over her head and shoulders. Her companion also wears a pleated farji under a short jama. The couple are shown smoking a huqqa.

A Muslim Couple, ca. 1780

The man wears a cotton jama with a decorative self-buttoned closure; it is belted with a sash that has been tucked in and draped across the back. In his belt is a katar. The woman is dressed in a choli, with the ghaghra tucked under the bottom. She wears a short sari that forms a skirt.

Court Musician and Dancer, ca. 1790

The musician (left) wears a cotton jama over isar. The sash around his waist is used to support his *vina* (stringed instrument). The dancer (right) wears a choli with a sheer ghaghra caught under its band (the traditional front panel has evolved into a tassel). Draped over her arm is a sheer dopatta, edged with pearls.

Woman from Bombay [now Mumbai]
Nineteenth and Twentieth Centuries

This woman is a resident of Bombay (now known as Mumbai). By the nineteenth century, the sari had become the garment of choice for most Indian women; their status was indicated by—among other things—the richness of the sari's fabric.

Man of Bombay
Nineteenth and Twentieth Centuries

The jama survived into modern times, becoming knee length; here it is worn over puttees and sandals. The man's turban is wound around a cloth taj. He carries a chhattar.

Female Day Laborer
Nineteenth and Twentieth Centuries

This woman is a day laborer, also known as a coolie. She wears a choli with a dhoti, and a dopatta, which is tucked into the waistband and draped over her head. She wears simple jewelry: modest bangles, anklets, and a necklace.

26

Footman or House Boy, Bombay
Nineteenth and Twentieth Centuries

This type of footman, or house boy, could be found in Bombay from the nineteenth century to the present. A knee-length kurta is worn with a sash at the waist; it is accessorized with a large-brimmed felt hat. Many men's coats and jackets were white; white garments carried religious significance, as white represents purity of spirit.

Poona Gardener
Nineteenth and Twentieth Centuries

This simply attired gardener is from Poona (the old spelling for Pune), a city on the central-western coast of India. He wears a closely fitted jacket and shorts that are appropriate to his work in the garden.

Bombay Businessman
Nineteenth and Twentieth Centuries

A businessman from Bombay is pictured wearing a short, colorful jacket held closed by a waist sash. The sash and pleated skirt are made of the same fabric. He wears a tall lattice-pattern hat.

Bombay Businessman
Nineteenth and Twentieth Centuries

A Bombay businessman wears a knee-length jama with a waist sash over a dhoti. Over his shoulders is a shawl. His dome-like hat is a type of fez, or tarboosh.

Bombay Businessman
Nineteenth and Twentieth Centuries

A businessman is dressed in layers consisting of a knee-length kurta worn over a shirt, with a broad sash; underneath is a wraparound sarong-like skirt. He wears a broad-brimmed hat and turned-up slippers.

Women of Maharashtra
Nineteenth and Twentieth Centuries

These two women are from the state of Maharashtra in west-central India. They wear the skirts of their saris pulled through their legs in the manner of the dhoti. The woman on the right wears a thick bangle and anklets.

Ceylon Official and Wife
Nineteenth and Twentieth Centuries

The people of Ceylon (now Sri Lanka) have a distinctive costume, the shirt-like garment called a comboy. The length and width of the comboy indicate the wearer's social class. The man's comboy is full length and has been wrapped around the figure and gathered into the belt in the front. He wears a short, puffed-sleeve bolero jacket. The woman's shorter comboy is worn over a sarong-wrapped sari.

Tamil Couple
Nineteenth and Twentieth Centuries

The man and woman display the costume of the Tamil inhabitants of north Ceylon and south India. The man wears a belted sarong. The woman is dressed in a short-sleeved cotton kurta with a sarong that has been pulled around the waist to form a sash. She wears a festival headdress.

Devil Dancer and Drummer
Nineteenth and Twentieth Centuries

A devil dancer, from one of India's many festivals, is pictured with his drummer. The dancer wears a lion mask, the *kirttimukha*, representing the god Shiva. His costume consists of a gold-braided jacket worn over a vest.

His overskirt is made of the same fabric as the vest and is also gold trimmed. The drummer wears a sarong and a loosely wrapped pagri, or turban.

Professional Dancing Girls
Nineteenth and Twentieth Centuries

These professional dancing girls, shown here performing in a mirror image, were known as *nautch*. Their costume consists of choli, ghaghra, and dopatta. They wear jeweled girdles around their hips. Both wear simple necklaces, bangles, anklets, and floral hair ornaments.

Jodhpur Lancer
Early Twentieth Century

A jodhpur lancer is shown in his distinctive uniform. Jodhpur, a former state in northwest India (now part of Rajasthan), lent its name to riding breeches with a dis- tinctive silhouette—cut full at the hips and tightly fitting from the knee to the ankle. He wears leather knee boots and a pagri.

Sikh Family
Twentieth Century

Sikh men wear the turban at all times according to their religious beliefs. The man is dressed in a kurta, which he wears under a sleeveless vest. Sikh women generally wear a kurta over chouridar, and they cover their heads with a dopatta (this combination is known as a "Punjabi suit"). The child wears a short-sleeved kurta in a patterned cotton print.

Workmen
Twentieth Century

The two workmen standing at the left wear variations of the kurta; the man on the far left wears jodhpurs, and the man beside him is dressed in a long dhoti. The worker on the right wears a short dhoti. All wear loosely tied turbans, or pagri.

Method of Folding a Dhoti

1. Grasp the ends of the fabric, A & B, and pull them forward, about a foot from the body, to find the center. **2.** Folding from the center, tie the end corners, A & B, at the left side. **3.** Catch the edge, E, of the left opening just above the knee and pull it over to the right, tucking it into the waist. **4.** Pick up the corner, C; pull back between the legs, fold the end into several pleats, and tuck the pleated end into the center of the back waistband. **5.** Pick up the end, D; fold into several pleats and pull up from about the center, tucking into the front waistband and allowing the free end to hang in the manner of a loincloth.

Method of Draping a Sari

1. Grasp the right end of the fabric and tuck it into the right side of the petticoat's waistband. (Note: The petticoat must have a drawstring at the waist; otherwise, it will not hold the sari securely.) **2.** Wrap the fabric around the waist, tucking it into the petticoat's waistband as you go until you reach the point on the right where you started. Starting here, make several deep pleats and tuck into the waistband. **3.** Lift up the free end. **4.** Draw it across the bosom, draping and arranging on the shoulder. The end also can be brought over the head to form a hood. **5.** The final look of the basic sari drape.

Couple in Formal Dress, 1960s

Here is a couple representative of the mid-twentieth century. The woman wears a luxurious silk sari with a gold lace choli. Her companion is dressed in a formal long "Nehru" coat with matching trousers and cap.

Today's "Nehru" is worn a bit longer—to the middle of the shin; the one shown is in the style of the 1960s. They both wear modern footwear.

Two Views of an Ensemble
Twentieth Century

At the left is a traditional silk kurta worn over darker silk salwar; both are embroidered with metallic thread. On the right is an outfit of a contemporary silk kurta worn over silk salwar. A silk dopatta drapes the shoulders.

Indian Family, ca. 2000

Shown here, at the turn of the twenty-first century, is a contemporary Indian family. The girl wears a multicolor-patterned choli with dark cotton salwar. The father wears a brightly colored silk shirt with dark trousers, both in western style. In a nod to tradition, the mother wears a jewel-toned silk sari with gold brocade trim and pattern.

Mumbai Fashions—Formal Wear, ca. 2000

Contemporary fashions of Mumbai, formerly Bombay, are pictured. At the left is an outfit consisting of a gold lace vest and full skirt with matching dopatta, worn with a low-cut choli. On the right is a modern printed-silk sari combined with a solid-color choli and skirt.

MOGHUL 17th C.

MOGHUL 17th C.

MADRAS, 17th C.

COURTESAN 19th C.

RAJASTHAN - 20th C.

HIMACHAL PRADESH 20th C.

RAJASTHAN 20th C.

BOMBAY 20th C.

HENNA HAND DECORATION.

BOMBAY 20th C.

HYDERBAD. (MUSLIM BRIDE), 20th C.

JEWELED BRAID 17th C. TO PRESENT.

Women's Hairstyles, Headdresses, and Jewelry

46

Various Turbans of the Nineteenth and Twentieth Centuries

COOLIE
19-20th C.

KASHMIR
19-20th C.

KASHMIR
19-20th C.

MADRAS
19-20th C.

MADRAS
19-20th C.

BENGAL (BRIDEGROOM)
20th C.

PUSHKAR
20th C.

JAIPUR POLICEMAN
20th C.

BRAHMIN-BENGAL
19-20th C.

RAJASTHAN
OFFICER
20th C.

DHAR
OFFICIAL
L. 19th C.

BOY'S CROCHET
CAP.
PUSHKAR
20th C.

JODPHUR
FAKIR
20th C.

MAHARAJA
OF PATIALA.
SARPECH (BROOCH)
OF EMERALD &
PEARL
E. 20th C.

COSTUME FROM "RAMAYAN" - 20th C.

DIVAN OF
PAKANPUR
E. 20th C.

Various Men's Turbans and Shoe Styles of the Nineteenth and Twentieth Centuries